Where Do Ideas Come From?

Spectacular story starters, study guides and classroom resources

By

Simon Rose

Where Do Ideas Come From?
Copyright © 2016 by Simon Rose
Second edition copyright © 2025

Published by Sorcerer's Letterbox Publishing
Calgary, Alberta
www.simon-rose.com

Print and Ebook layout by Ryah Deines

Contents

Introduction

Many of my novels can be used as the basis for workshops and projects in the classroom. *The Alchemist's Portrait, The Sorcerer's Letterbox,* and *The Heretic's Tomb* are all time travel stories and can be used as the basis for workshops in which students create time machines and stories set in a different era. All three novels are also ideal for studying the different historical periods depicted in the stories.

The Alchemist's Portrait can be the starting point for workshops using pictures for inspiration, creating stories based on artifacts found in museums, or for creating unique characters. *The Sorcerer's Letterbox* might inspire children to learn more about the Tower of London or other medieval castles, as well as study the mystery of the Princes in the Tower, the Wars of the Roses, and medieval life.

The Heretic's Tomb can be used to learn about the Black Death, medieval society, the beginnings of healthcare, or the role of the medieval church. There are also strong female characters in the story, and this can lead to students learning more about the very important women that lived in the Middle Ages. Teachers can use *The Clone Conspiracy* as a starting point for projects about the development of technology or what students might expect to see in the world of the future. *The Emerald Curse* is an excellent novel for projects in which the students create their own superheroes and comic books.

The Doomsday Mask can be used to study ancient civilizations, ruined cities, and the extinctions of animals that took place at the end of the Ice Age. *The Time Camera* lends itself to wonderful projects related to the history of photography, writing speculative stories about alternate history, and finding inspiration from old photographs. *The Sphere of Septimus* has a wealth of potential for projects in which students create their own fantasy kingdoms, along with the people and animals that inhabit their imaginary world.

Simon Rose

Where Do Ideas Come From? provides suggestions and recommendations for teachers developing classroom projects based on all the novels but might also serve as inspiration for aspiring writers of all ages.

Chapter One
The Alchemist's Portrait

A school trip to the art gallery at the city museum leads Matthew into an eerie meeting with Peter Glimmer, imprisoned inside his own portrait by his villainous uncle in 1666. Entrusted by Peter with recovering the one object that can save the world, Matthew is sent hurtling over 300 years into the past. Encountering magic, mayhem and murder, Matthew also has to contend with Peter's uncle, the ruthless and seemingly immortal Nicolaas van der Leyden, at every turn, in a desperate race through time to save the future.

Character creation

In *The Alchemist's Portrait*, Matthew's adventure begins following a trip to the local art gallery located inside a museum. Portraits or even photographs can be an excellent starting point for character creation exercises. Children can create a character based on their impression of the individual in the picture, adding in different personality traits.

Mannerisms and habits

Family and friends

Occupation and education

Favourite foods and drinks

Pets and hobbies

Life experiences

Many more items could be added to this list and the students should be encouraged to use whatever they feel makes their chosen character more realistic and believable.

Historical eras

In the novel, Matthew's travels in time transport

him to specific historical periods, some involving dramatic events that provide a host of great ideas for student projects.

The French Revolution

The American Civil War

The Russian Revolution

Matthew also visits Amsterdam in 1666, which could serve as the basis for studying some aspects of this particular time period.

The Flemish school of art, which produced many famous artists and paintings

The Dutch East India Company's international trade and commerce

European expansion around the world following the Age of Discovery

There are links to websites about all these time

periods, plus those related to the history of alchemy, at www.simon-rose.com on the page concerning the historical background of *The Alchemist's Portrait*.

Time travel tales

*T*he *Alchemist's Portrait* is about time travel, which has been a popular theme in books and movies for a long time and continues to be popular.

Using the novel as inspiration, children can devise their own time travel machines, devices or methods, devising a way to travel back in time and return safely home again. They can then incorporate this into a time travel story. Here are a few things for the students to consider when creating their adventure.

What time travel methods do they know of from books, television and movies?

What types of research do they need to do when writing a story set in the past?

If they could travel back in time, where would they visit in the past?

Why would they go to that particular place in history?

How would they get there and how would they return home safely?

When they create a means of traveling back in time, students must be very specific regarding how it works. The method has to be believable and fully explained, rather than a character simply pressing a button, pulling a lever, or making a wish to travel into the past. The device or method has to be plausible in order for the story to make sense.

Doorways and portals

In *The Alchemist's Portrait*, Matthew travels in time by using the frame of the portrait of Nicolaas van der Leyden as a portal between different historical eras. This lends itself to some ideas for creative writing projects.

For example, children might imagine that

they're in the school library, searching for an elusive book, perhaps one that they really need to complete a project. They notice a strange door that they've never seen before and for some reason are compelled to open the door and step through it. Where would it take them?

Another time

A different dimension

An alien planet

A parallel universe

This is merely a suggestion, and portals and doorways could be situated just about anywhere, with endless possibilities for stories.

Museum mysteries

In the novel, Matthew's initial meeting with Peter Glimmer takes place in the art gallery at the local museum, which has collections not only of paintings but also ancient Egyptian artifacts, suits of armour, and historical objects from many different eras. After a school field trip to a museum, there are many ideas that can serve as story starters.

A time travel story based on one of the objects at the museum

A mystery story featuring the theft of one of the museum's exhibits

A writing project about how an object may have been used in the past

Conducting research into an item's historical era

There are certainly lots of possibilities, all based on the students' favourite memories from their excursion.

The art of inspiration

The world of fine art is one of the themes of *The Alchemist's Portrait*. Pictures often serve as a source of inspiration for writers and paintings other than portraits can also be used to devise creative writing projects.

Have the students select a piece of artwork and write a short story about it, based on their own perception of the picture they're studying. It's usually quite remarkable to see what children can devise during this process. Depending on the number of students in a group, only a limited number of images might be able to be used in a session. In this case, it's always interesting to see the widely different stories two or more children come up with, based on their impression of the same picture.

Chapter Two
The Sorcerer's Letterbox

In a hidden drawer in the base of an old wooden box, Jack discovers a letter from a boy calling himself Edward. Penning a reply, Jack is astonished to be corresponding through time with the boy king Edward V, one of the famous Princes in the Tower, murdered by King Richard III. Traveling back in time, Jack attempts to rescue Edward V and his brother from their fate, but is soon fighting for his life in the terrifying London of 1483.

In *The Sorcerer's Letterbox*, Jack travels back in time to the late Middle Ages for an exciting adventure based on actual events and featuring real characters from history. The novel can be used as the basis for a wide variety of creative writing projects.

The Wars of the Roses

The Sorcerer's Letterbox is set during the final years of the Wars of the Roses, which took place during some of the most tumultuous decades in the history of medieval England. Student projects could include detailed research into this fascinating era.

The intricate political events of the time

The ambitions of the various branches of the rival royal families

The deadly plots of kings and queens

The tragic life of Edward V, who became king when he was only fourteen years old

The Tower of London

This formidable fortress is one of the world's leading tourist attractions and a World Heritage site. The Tower plays a major role in *The Sorcerer's Letterbox* and is a great topic for student projects.

Research into the fascinating history of the Tower of London

Learn about castles and other medieval fortifications

Medieval warfare, weaponry and battle strategies

The justice system in the Middle Ages

There are links to websites about this time period, plus those related to the Tower of London, at www.simon-rose.com on the page related to the historical background of *The Sorcerer's Letterbox*.

Medieval detectives

The famous story of the Princes in the Tower has often been described as history's greatest murder mystery. Many theories have been advanced, with most historians believing that Richard III had his nephews murdered before seizing the crown of

England for himself. However, many other intriguing possibilities remain for assignments.

Conducting an investigation into the disappearance of the princes in 1483

Investigating Richard III's possible motives

Research into the other suspects in the mystery

Studies of forensic techniques used in modern police investigations

There are links to websites about the Princes in the Tower, plus a link to my video about the story behind the story of *The Sorcerer's Letterbox*, at www.simon-rose.com.

Life in the Middle Ages

The Sorcerer's Letterbox takes place in 1483, towards the end of the Middle Ages. This can provide the basis for countless projects regarding the later medieval period.

Simon Rose

Daily life in the Middle Ages

Literature and culture

The early years of the Renaissance

Medieval architecture

The origins of the Reformation

The history of the famous London Bridge

The impact on Europe of the voyages of Columbus

At www.simon-rose.com, there are links to websites related to the historical background of *The Sorcerer's Letterbox*.

The world of words

The mysterious scroll Jack studies at the beginning of the story is written in Middle English, one of the many versions of the English language that existed before the modern era. This could provide the framework for a study of the way the language has evolved, and how modern English differs from that spoken in medieval times.

Incredible journeys

In *The Sorcerer's Letterbox*, Jack's own incredible journey into the past begins following his discovery of a mysterious medieval wooden box. Students could be asked to imagine where such a magic box might take them in history. They could also use a different ancient object as their starting point for an exciting time travel story.

Chapter Three
The Clone Conspiracy

At the dawn of the twenty-first century, nervous governments around the world reacted quickly to pass legislation banning human cloning. Panicked as technology rapidly advanced, they didn't realize that the genetic genie had already escaped from the bottle. When Luke's best friend Patrick vanishes and the police quickly close the case, Luke is determined to uncover the truth. Tantalizing clues lead Luke and Patrick's sister Emma to LennoxGen, where they stumble across a shocking international conspiracy with catastrophic consequences for the future of mankind.

The Clone Conspiracy involves secret experiments, unethical scientists, government cover-ups, human cloning, and genetic engineering. Here's just a selection of projects that could be generated from the novel.

Clone for a day

Imagine if you had a clone for the day. What use would you make of a duplicate of yourself over the course of twenty-four hours?

Send the clone to school or work on your behalf

Do things you've always wanted to do but never had the opportunity

Devise ways to keep your clone a secret from your friends and family

Consider what complications might occur if the clone didn't behave as expected

This exercise can really tap into the students' creative energy, as they explore the many possible hypothetical scenarios.

Medical marvels

Human cloning has been the topic of many stories, TV shows, and movies over the years. However, some aspects of the technology could have many potential benefits for mankind.

How might cloning be applied to current medical procedures?

What are the pros and cons of developing cloning technology?

In what ways might cloning help combat incurable diseases and medical conditions

Are there any potential future medical inventions that currently seem like science fiction

Future technology

Students could explore potential inventions that may transform the way we live in the coming decades. Children can invent an imaginary product, which could be related to transportation, medical, sports, entertainment, lifestyle, habitat, or even household appliances. Students can then explain more about their product.

What are the product's features and benefits?

Design a newspaper or magazine advertisement for the product

Write the script for a radio commercial

Create a product's TV commercial, which can be performed as a skit

In each instance, the commercials must be exciting and sufficiently effective to sell the product to potential customers.

Making mammoths

Children are usually familiar with the premise of Jurassic Park. However, they may not be as knowledgeable about the serious attempts to use frozen mammoth bodies to attempt to recreate these long extinct beasts, with the help of DNA from modern elephants. There is also ongoing research into how current animal species threatened with extinction might survive with the assistance of technologies developed from cloning. This could form the basis of a number of classroom projects.

Discussions about the ethics of using cloning to resurrect long dead creatures

Research into extinct species, other than dinosaurs, that may be revived

Examining current threatened animals that might be helped by cloning technology

Chapter Four
The Emerald Curse

Charles Kelly was the world's greatest comic book artist, until he disappeared without a trace. Two years later, his grandson Sam discovers a mysterious pen in Kelly's attic studio. Sam is soon propelled into a bizarre dimension, where super villains are all powerful and disturbingly real, and finds himself in a deadly confrontation with an evil entity, imprisoned inside a mystical gemstone since the dawn of time.

In *The Emerald Curse*, Sam has adventures inside a strange comic book universe. The novel can inspire a range of student projects related to the superhero genre and the wonderful world of comic books.

Create your own superhero

In this exercise, students invent a superhero. Most children are familiar with the superhero genre and are aware of what they need to include when creating their heroic character.

An appropriate name and a colourful costume

Amazing powers, weapons, or devices used to fight crime

A secret identity

Friends and family

A secret headquarters

An archenemy

Students could also craft detailed character outlines for their hero, along with all the supporting players, including their main adversary and even a sidekick.

26

The origin

Once they have invented their superhero, the students can create an exciting origin story, detailing how the hero initially gained his or her powers.

Most superheroes the students are familiar with, such as Spider-Man or Batman, have very distinctive origin tales in which they acquired their powers or were inspired to become heroes and children really enjoy creating these stories. For example, students could create a superhero origin story with a distinct beginning, middle, and end.

The beginning deals with the character's ordinary daily life, before the event that gave them superpowers and changed them forever

In the middle the character discovers, perhaps by accident when recovering in hospital, that they have superhuman abilities

At the conclusion the character decides to become a hero, devises a costume and perhaps weapons, builds a secret base, and vows to fight crime

Headline news

In the style of a traditional newspaper's front page, students can write an exciting, dramatic story, describing a battle between the hero and his archenemy. Students can research other front-page newspaper stories to generate ideas for their story.

An attention-grabbing headline

An action-packed story describing the battle as it happened

Quotes from witnesses who are questioned by reporters

Interviews with the chief of police after the villain's defeat

In addition to the catchy headline, the story should make effective use of descriptive words to convey a vivid picture of all the action that took place.

Comic books

The Emerald Curse was inspired by the superhero comics I read while growing up. Comic books can provide many ideas for student projects.

The storyline in *The Emerald Curse* could be transformed into a comic book, using the illustrations that are scattered throughout the text as a starting point. Students can create their own comic book, depicting an adventure starring the superhero they've created

The covers of comic books are always very distinctive, and this can form the basis of a separate student project. Covers are usually action-packed, depicting the hero fighting an adversary, flying through the night above the city skyline, and so on. Students will have their own ideas, but here are a few general guidelines for crafting comic covers.

Lots of action to grab the reader's attention and drag them into the story

Large lettering in imposing blocks for the

hero's name, usually taking up at least a third of the cover

If it's the first ever issue, it can be called something like 'Introducing the Amazing Spider-Man'

A different title might be something along the lines of 'The Return of Doctor Octopus' or 'The Joker Strikes Again'

The comic's price, date and issue number

Board games

In the novel, Sam is propelled into the comic book universe and has adventures in several different worlds, before arriving in the realm ruled by the evil Baron Midnight.

Sam's travels into the comic book illustrations and subsequent journeys elsewhere in the superhero dimension could form the basis of a board game. Students could develop this once they're familiar with the storyline of *The Emerald Curse.*

Chapter Five
The Heretic's Tomb

While exploring a medieval archaeological site containing the ruins of an ancient English abbey, Annie discovers the long-forgotten tomb of Lady Isabella Devereaux, who had been condemned to death as a heretic in 1349. When Annie curiously examines a mysterious amulet she finds in the tomb, she is suddenly sent hurtling back to the Middle Ages, encountering sorcery, treachery, treason and the ghastly horrors of the Black Death.

The Heretic's Tomb takes place in England in 1349 at the height of the Black Death, which is estimated to have killed between thirty and forty percent of the population, or approximately two million people. In Europe as a whole, it is estimated that more than 25 million perished as a result of the devastating plague between 1347 and 1351.

The Black Death

The great plague of the mid-fourteenth century offers a wealth of opportunities for student projects.

Research into the disease, its causes and effects

Medieval medicine, scientific knowledge, and doctors

The effects of the Black Death on society at the time

The Black Death as a factor in later developments, such as the decline of feudalism and the Peasants Revolt of 1381

At www.simon-rose.com, you can find details and links regarding the Black Death and medieval medicine.

Ancient artifacts

In *The Heretic's Tomb*, Annie's means of time travel is an artifact from the Middle Ages, which can provide themes for student projects.

The discovery of a long-forgotten object with the power to travel in time

The object may not be a time travel device, but something that plays a major role in a story set in a particular time period

An object with incredible powers, such as the power to conquer death possessed by the medallion in *The Heretic's Tomb*

The artifact could also simply serve as the starting point for a story

Uncovering the past

In the chapters of *The Heretic's Tomb* set in the present day, Annie explores an archaeological site in London. Students could study this aspect of archaeology and learn more about its connection to the story.

Different types of archaeological excavations

The techniques and equipment used in studying excavated sites

Items that might be uncovered during excavations

Famous archeological sites around the world, such as those in Italy, Greece, the Middle East, and elsewhere

The Middle Ages

The Heretic's Tomb takes place in the mid-fourteenth century and the history of the medieval period has a great deal of potential for student projects.

The Hundred Years War

The reigns of Edward II, Edward III, and Richard II

The Peasants Revolt

Medieval warfare, knights, and chivalry

Feudalism and systems of government

Medieval society and living conditions

There are links to websites about the medieval period at www.simon-rose.com on the pages dealing with the historical background of *The Heretic's Tomb*.

The medieval church

The church was a formidable presence in medieval society. The church's influence over people's daily lives is evident throughout *The Heretic's Tomb*. Students could study this important element of the story in order to better understand the time period.

The role of the church in the Middle Ages

How monasteries and convents operated

The construction of Europe's majestic cathedrals

Medieval heretical movements and the seeds of the Reformation

On the pages dealing with the historical background to *The Heretic's Tomb* at www.simon-rose.com, there are links to websites about the medieval period.

Girl power

The Middle Ages is often seen as an era dominated by the daring and heroic exploits of men. However, students could also learn about prominent medieval women.

Eleanor of Aquitaine

Isabella of France

Margaret of Anjou

Joan of Arc

Lady Isabella Devereaux is one of the leading characters in *The Heretic's Tomb* and many women were important in this era.

The history of books

Two books from antiquity feature in *The Heretic's Tomb*. Student projects could involve the development of the written word.

Scrolls used in the ancient world

Parchments illustrated and embellished by monks in medieval monasteries

The origins of bound copies of books

The invention of printing and its effect on medieval society

Chapter Six
The Doomsday Mask

The legendary crystal ceremonial mask of Kulkaan, high priest of Atlantis, was believed to have been endowed with incredible powers. In the ancient civilization's destruction, the mask was thought to have been shattered and irretrievably lost, eventually being forgotten. Long considered to be a mere myth, the mask's crystal fragments have now been found and the mask of Kulkaan reassembled, with deadly consequences for all mankind. In a desperate race against time, Josh and Erica must prevent the mask from falling intact into the hands of the shadowy Crystalline Order to save the world from catastrophe.

The *Doomsday Mask* features the legend of Atlantis, stolen treasure in World War II, mysteries of Central America, and prophecies about the end of the world, all great topics on which to base student projects.

The end of World War II

The opening chapter of *The Doomsday Mask* takes place in Berlin during the chaos at the end of World War II. Large parts of the city were destroyed and the army recruited anyone strong enough to hold a weapon in the waning days of the war, including children. Art treasures and other valuables were stolen by the Nazis from all over Europe. One treasure horde hidden in a mine contained thousands of bags of gold, silver, and valuable coins worth over $500 million, along with jewelry and priceless works of art. Students can explore many different aspects of this era.

What life was like for children during World War II

How children served as soldiers during the conflict

The kinds of valuable objects that were stolen during the war

The types of treasure found by Allied armies in the final days of the fighting

The legend of Atlantis

The Mask of Kulkaan featured in *The Doomsday Mask* is an ancient crystal artifact and a remnant of Atlantis. The legendary city can be the inspiration for a number of projects.

Legends about Atlantis, the city, and its civilization

Theories about how Atlantis may have been destroyed

Plate tectonics and the Earth's shifting surface

Theories about where the city may have been located, if it existed

Crystal skulls and other mysteries of Central America

The Pleistocene Extinction

Paleontologists suspect that a catastrophic event occurred 12,000 years ago, or around 10,000 BC, which is about the same time as the supposed destruction of Atlantis.

Vast numbers of large mammals such as mammoths, mastodons, saber tooth tigers and others vanished almost overnight in what was known as the Pleistocene Extinction. Here are a few ideas for student projects on this topic.

The types of animals that existed at the end of the Pleistocene

Other theories about the great extinction that occurred at this time

Other major extinctions, other than those related to dinosaurs

Species that have become extinct in recent

centuries

The threat of extinction faced by some species in the modern era

Ancient cities of the Americas

The ancient cities of Central and South America served as inspiration for *The Doomsday Mask*.

The city of Tenochtitlan, established in 1325 and the capital of the Aztec Empire

Teotihuacan, one of the most visited archaeological sites in Mexico

Chichen Itza, built by the Mayan civilization in the Yucatan peninsular

Tiahuanaco, located near Lake Titicaca in Bolivia

Machu Picchu, the lost city of the Incas, located high in the Peruvian Andes

Where Do Ideas Come From?

The Doomsday Mask historical background page on my website has links to online resources about World War II, Atlantis, mysteries of the Americas, ancient cities, and the Pleistocene Extinction at www.simon-rose.com.

Chapter Seven
The Time Camera

The massive explosion in which Eleanor Chamberlain died at her research laboratory was widely seen as a tragic accident. Or was it the perfect crime?

Two years later, Jake and Lydia discover a mysterious camera, capable of taking pictures of the distant past and more ominously, of the future. As they uncover the shocking truth and learn of secrets that someone will kill to protect, Jake and Lydia are soon propelled into a deadly and desperate race against time in order to save the future.

The Time Camera is an exciting adventure involving incredible inventions, the development of an advanced form of camera, time travel, and the ability to photograph both past and future events. It can form the basis for projects related to digital cameras, photography, and computer editing, but also inspire a number of creative writing exercises.

The History of Photography

Children often don't realize how long photography has been around and can research the history of the technology.

The development of photography in the early nineteenth century

The different types of early photographic processes

Early portraits of prominent people

Spirit photography and hoax pictures

History's most famous photographs

What if?

In the novel, pictures are taken of the future, allowing people to become wealthy due to their knowledge of coming events. This could provide inspiration for a variety of student writing projects.

Inventing future newspaper headlines for important events

Imagining daily life fifty years in the future

Considering how far into the future they might want to travel and why

Changing the past

In *The Time Camera*, Lydia and Jake use the camera to travel into the past in an attempt to prevent the death of Lydia's mother. This concept can be a great starting point for students to explore the complexities involved in manipulating previous events.

Where would you go if you could travel into the recent past?

Which historical events would you change if you had the power to do so?

What problems might result from altering the past?

Every picture tells a story

Photographs can provide wonderful inspiration for creative writing projects. In this exercise, children select some general photographs featuring people and situations to use as story starters, giving full reign to their imaginations to create a story from their picture.

What do you think is going on in the picture?

Who are the people in the picture and how are they connected to each other?

What might have led up to this scene and what might happen next?

What might be happening outside the borders of the picture?

Whatever picture the students choose, they'll be sure to develop impressive story ideas. They'll also often have very different interpretations of identical photographs. This exercise in creative writing really stimulates your students' imagination, whatever form that may take.

Chapter Eight
The Sphere of Septimus

Eric isn't too happy when he has to spend the summer with his eccentric father, Septimus Trinket, in the backwater village of Middle Wogglehole, deep in the heart of rural Derbyshire. In the isolated village, however, things are not quite what they seem. Eric meets Jessica, who tells him of the legends and mysterious stories that have surrounded Middle Wogglehole for centuries. When they discover Septimus' shocking secret, Eric and Jessica are soon fighting for their lives against the forces of evil, in a world very different to their own.

The Sphere of Septimus takes place in the small English village of Middle Wogglehole and also in Koronada, a fictional realm with a number of different kingdoms inhabited by a variety of unusual characters and mythological creatures.

Exercises related to the novel involve students creating their own fantasy kingdom. Students can also invent their own unique mythological creature, along with its powers, enemies, diet, and habitat.

Marvelous maps

In this exercise, children create a physical map of their imaginary country, highlighting the terrain and natural resources. Students can study an atlas of the world or maps of different countries for some ideas. Children might wish to create an entire world with several different continents or one large island.

Some of the things that could be featured on the map include:

Bays

Estuaries

Canyons

Deserts

Grasslands

Islands

Lakes

Mountains

Peninsulas

Polar regions

Oceans and seas

Rivers

Swamps

Volcanoes

Flags and banners

All countries have flags, banners and emblems, usually depicting something significant from the country's history. However, some symbols such as lions, eagles, swords, horses, and even flowers are quite common. In this exercise, students design a flag or banner for their country and explain why the country's rulers chose it.

Government, people, and economy

In this exercise, students add more details about their fictional country.

What is the climate like? Is it temperate, tropical, or cold?

Who is in charge and who are the country's rulers?

What is the system of government and where is the capital city?

Are there other large cities, towns and major ports?

What is the economy like? Does the country have any natural resources and if so, what are they used for?

What is the currency called and what do the coins and bills look like?

What about major roads and other means of transportation?

These are simply a few suggestions, but students can always come up with others to paint a more detailed picture of their imaginary country.

Amazing artifacts and magical objects

The Sphere of Septimus features a mysterious crystal sphere with incredible powers. Students might like to craft an adventure story featuring a unique mysterious artifact with wondrous abilities, a curse or a deadly secret.

A coin or medallion from an ancient civilization?

A ceremonial mask discovered in a ruined temple?

A gemstone unearthed in a long lost tomb?

The artifact could be a weapon, part of a statue, a valuable piece of jewelry, or a gemstone.

Children need to explain where the artifact originally came from, the myths and legends associated with it, any special powers it possesses or an unusual aspect that gives it great significance. Students can create an exciting, fast-paced tale featuring adventurers, explorers, scientists, secret societies, treasure maps, perhaps even a race against time to save the world.

Fantasy creatures

Most people are very familiar with monsters and strange creatures from mythology, books and movies, such as centaurs, unicorns, minotaurs, dragons, and so many others. In this exercise students create their own unique mythological creature, combining two other animals. Students will need to describe the creature's appearance and possibly draw a picture.

What is the creature's habitat like?

Does it live in the desert, the mountains, the forest, swamps, lakes, in the ocean, or somewhere else?

What does it eat?

How long does the creature live and does it lay eggs or give birth to live young?

What special powers does the creature possess?

Does it have any enemies?

Culture, myths, and legends

Countries around the world have distinctive cultures and traditions that distinguish them from other nations. There are many of these that might be invented for an imaginary country.

Is the cuisine made from local plants, animals, and other ingredients?

Is there something distinctive about the country's music or the instruments on which it is played?

Are there dances or theatrical performances that are performed at ceremonies to mark historical events, a declaration of independence, the anniversary of an important battle, or the death of a renowned ruler?

Are there certain kinds of clothes that are worn or does the country have a national costume?

Is there a national sport or game?

What different people inhabit the imaginary kingdom? What are they like and how do they differ from each other?

What myths and legends are important to the country's people?

Does the country have any enemies? If so, how did they become an adversary of the country?

Tourism guide

Once all the details regarding the imaginary country are established, students can create a brief tourist guide to their imaginary country. What sort of things would attract someone to travel to the country?

The climate, the wildlife, or the beaches?

The cultural richness enjoyed by those living in the nation's cities?

What about souvenirs and shopping?

The objective of the tourism guide is to encourage people to visit the country and contribute to its economy.

Conclusion

For many authors of novels for children and young adults there's the opportunity to create study guides, workshops, and classroom resources influenced by the plot, themes, or characters in a book, no matter what the genre. Assignments and projects based on a story that the students have read and enjoyed help to generate interest in both reading and writing. A novel might also inspire children to create their own unique stories.

The suggestions and recommendations outlined in *Where Do Ideas Come From?* provide both established and aspiring authors with advice and ideas designed to spark creativity. For published authors considering ways to promote their own novels as classroom resources, this book serves as an excellent starting point. The author is the person most familiar with the plot and characters in a novel and how these might be employed to inspire and motivate others in their own writing and creative endeavors, no matter what form that may take.

Wherever your creative path takes you, enjoy the journey.

About the Author

Simon Rose's first novel for middle-grade readers, *The Alchemist's Portrait*, was published in 2003, followed by *The Sorcerer's Letterbox* in 2004, *The Clone Conspiracy* in 2005, *The Emerald Curse* in 2006, *The Heretic's Tomb* in 2007, *The Doomsday Mask* in 2009, *The Time Camera* in 2011, *The Sphere of Septimus* in 2014, *Flashback* in 2015, *Future Imperfect* in 2016, *Twisted Fate* and the *Shadowzone* series in 2017, *Parallel Destiny* in 2018, *The Stone of the Seer* series in 2022, and *An Untimely Death* in 2024

Simon is also the author of *The Children's Writer's Guide, The Working Writer's Guide, The*

Social Media Writer's Guide, Where Do Ideas Come From?, The Time Traveler's Guide, The Children's Writer's Guide 2, a contributing author to *The Complete Guide to Writing Science Fiction,* and has written more than a hundred non-fiction books for children and young adults with Crabtree Publishing, Beech Street Books, True North, Capstone, and Weigl Educational Publishers.

Simon is a writing instructor at the University of Calgary and has served as the Writer-in-Residence for the Canadian Authors Association. Simon provides editing and coaching services for writers in a wide range of genres. You can view details of the references and recommendations regarding his work on his website.

Simon offers in-person and virtual programs for schools and libraries and offers a variety of online writing courses and workshops for both children and adults. He has extensive experience in writing for a wide range of industries and offers copywriting services for the business community.

Full details can be found on his website, www.simon-rose.com.

Books by Simon Rose

Fiction

The Alchemist's Portrait

The Sorcerer's Letterbox

The Clone Conspiracy

The Emerald Curse

The Heretic's Tomb

The Doomsday Mask

The Time Camera

The Sphere of Septimus

Future Imperfect

Flashback

Twisted Fate

Parallel Destiny

Shadowzone

Into the Web

Black Dawn

The Stone of the Seer

Royal Blood

Revenge of the Witchfinder

An Untimely Death

Non-fiction

The Time Traveler's Guide

Where Do Ideas Come From?

The Children's Writer's Guide

The Children's Writer's Guide 2

The Working Writer's Guide

The Social Media Writer's Guide

Exploring the Fantasy Realm

*School and Library Visits for Authors and
    Illustrators*

Amazing Animals: Belugas

Canadian Icons: Loonies

Remarkable People: Nelson Mandela

Canadian Icons: Canada's Olympic Torch

Meteors

Remarkable People: Aung San Suu Kyi

Sources of Light

What is Light?

Sea Urchins

Colosseum

Army

Navy

Air Force

Marine Corps

Simon Rose

Coast Guard

*The Split History of World War II: A
    Perspectives Flip Book*

CN Tower

Parliament Hill

Confederation Bridge

Does Canada Own the Arctic?

Tim Hortons

Air Force Special Operations

Marine Corps Special Operations

Army Rangers

Green Berets

Navy SEALs

Delta Force

Zapotecs

America at War: World War II

America at War: Vietnam

Ecosystems: Polar Ice Caps

Ecosystems: Estuaries

Ecosystems: Coral Reefs

Royal Bank of Canada

Canada in World War I: Roots of the Conflict

Canada in World War I: Battles

Canada in World War I: A Soldier's Life

Where Do Ideas Come From?

Canada in World War I: Life at Home

Canada in World War I: The Aftermath

America at War: Civil War

America at War: Revolutionary War

America at War: War of 1812

America at War: Mexican-American War

The Cardiovascular System

The Nervous System

The Skeletal System

The Respiratory System

The Digestive System

The Muscular System

Senate: U.S. Government

House of Representatives: U.S. Government

Supreme Court: U.S. Government

The Presidency: U.S. Government

House of Commons: Canada's Government

Senate: Canada's Government

Supreme Court: Canada's Government

The Crown: Canada's Government

One World Trade Centre

Oriental Pearl

Drones: Global Issues

Ticks

Simon Rose

First Settlers 1493-1606

Sheikh Zayed Grand Mosque

Harminder Sahib Sikh Temple

Dirty Jobs: Taxidermist

Dirty Jobs: Animal Caretaker

Dirty Jobs: Fisher

Dirty Jobs: Mechanic

Dirty Jobs: Plumber

Myths and Science of Astronomy: Ursa Major

Myths and Science of Astronomy: Pegasus

Myths and Science of Astronomy: Andromeda

Myths and Science of Astronomy: Orion

Myths and Science of Astronomy: Cygnus

Myths and Science of Astronomy: Hercules

Animal Adaptations: Resource Conservation

Animal Adaptations: Family Groups

Canada in World War II: Roots of the Conflict

Canada in World War II: Battles

Canada in World War II: A Soldier's Life

Canada in World War II: Life at Home

Canada in World War II: Aftermath

Canada in the World: NATO

Canada in the World: United Nations

Where Do Ideas Come From?

Canada in the World: World Health Organization

Canada in the World: World Trade Organization

Agricultural Drones

Indigenous Life in Canada: Truth and Reconciliation

Indigenous Life in Canada: Governance

Indigenous Life in Canada: Treaties

Indigenous Life in Canada: Spirituality

Heads Up! Concussion Awareness

Evaluating Arguments About Food

Evaluating Arguments About Animals

Evaluating Arguments About Technology

Evaluating Arguments About the Environment

Underground Transportation Systems

Indigenous Peoples in the World Wars

Indigenous Peoples in Politics

Amazing Volcanoes Around the World

Globes

Physical Maps

Horror in North Carolina

Canadian Celebrations - Christmas

Simon Rose

Canadian Celebrations - Canada Day

Canadian Celebrations - Halloween

Tsunami Readiness

Earthquake Readiness

First Nations, Metis, and Inuit Governance

Responsibilities of Citizenship

Canada's Political Parties

Healthy Kids Canada: Personal Safety

Healthy Kids Canada: Substances

Healthy Kids Canada: Embracing

Healthy Kids Canada: Real and Fictional Violence

Healthy Kids Canada: Gender Identity

Healthy Kids Canada: Growth and Development

Indigenous Life in Canada: Search for Clean Water

Indigenous Life in Canada: Racism and Stereotypes

Indigenous Life in Canada: Development of the Reserve System

Indigenous Life in Canada: Housing and Infrastructure

*Indigenous Life in Canada: Missing and
    Exploited Indigenous Women and Girls*

*Indigenous Life in Canada: Employment and
    Education*

War in Afghanistan

Battle of Vimy Ridge

Battle of the Somme

Battle of Juno Beach

Battle of the Atlantic

Battle of the Plains of Abraham

*Fight for Survival: Predator vs. Prey Coyote
vs. Field Mouse*

*Fight for Survival: Predator vs. Prey Grizzly
Bear vs. Salmon*

*Fight for Survival: Predator vs. Prey Lynx vs.
Snowshoe Hare*

*Fight for Survival: Predator vs. Polar Bear vs.
Ringed Seal*

*Fight for Survival: Predator vs. Prey Red Fox
vs. Red Squirrel*

*Fight for Survival: Predator vs. Prey Snowy
Owl vs. Lemming*

Anthologies

*The Complete Guide to Writing Science
Fiction Part One*

* List current as of 2025